Daily Devotional
For Leaders
(30–Day)

LaJoyce C. Harris

Daily Devotional for Leaders (30–Day)

Copyright ©2017 by LaJoyce C. Harris, All rights reserved.

Published by Milestone Publishing

Email: LajoyceHarris256@gmail.com

Printed in the United States of America

ISBN: 9781542925587

DEDICATION

This book is in loving memory of my mother, Esther Harris, one of the greatest prayer warriors and leaders who significantly impacted my life.

To my father, Pastor Joseph Harris, who watched me grow up and protected me. You have been a great father and I love you.

To my children, Yolanda, Patrick, and Justin, as well as my grandsons, Justin and Xander, and to Curtis—thank you guys for your love and support.

Contents

EDIFYING YOUR TEAM

Introduction

The strength of the group is in the will of the leader, and the will is character in action. ~Vince Lombardi

This devotional book is for leaders and leaders-in-training to help encourage you and hopefully jumpstart your day. Although it is written as a 30-day devotional, you can maximize it by taking one devotional a week and doing a study using the provided Scriptures and quotes. Each week spend some time seeing how you can apply a devotional to your daily life. Then the next week take the next devotional day and do the same. This way you are absorbing the material instead of just reading a new devotional every day without application.

Not sure you are a leader? Do not worry; there are many definitions of a leader. Below are some well-known quotes from some defining what a leader is:

The greatest leader is not necessarily the one who does the greatest things. He is the one that gets the people to do the greatest things. ~Ronald Reagan

Management is doing things right; leadership is doing the right things. ~Peter F. Drucker

Leadership is not about titles, positions, or flow charts. It is about one life influencing another. ~John C. Maxwell

One of the most important things about being a leader is you must see yourself leading or others will not. My prayer for you is that this devotional will help strengthen your prayer and study life, which can be building blocks to developing a strong leadership foundation.

Day One

Becoming Great

It shall not be so among you. But whoever would be great among you must be your servant. ~Matthew 20:26 (ESV)

Throughout Jesus' time on earth with His disciples, He taught them about greatness and humility. However, there are several passages where we read of them continuously trying to see who was the greatest among them, or who would be the greatest in the kingdom of God (Matthew 18:1; Luke 9:46).

> *After they arrived at Capernaum and settled in a house, Jesus asked his disciples, "What were you discussing out on the road?" But they didn't answer, because they had been arguing about which of them was the*

*greatest. He sat down, called the twelve disciples over to him, and said, "Whoever wants to be first must take last place and be the servant of everyone else." ~*Mark 9:33–35 (NLT)

Ecclesiastes 1:9 tells us that there is nothing new under the sun. Sometimes we forget that the disciples had to mature in their Christian walk, just like us. They had to learn to set aside their egos and grasp walking in humility, which seemingly was not easy for them to do. The above Scriptures reveal just how competitive the disciples were. On their way to minister, they argued over which one of them would be the greatest in the kingdom of God. It is amazing how man's definition of greatness is so different from God's. Knowing this, Jesus sat his disciples down and once again explained to them what greatness really is.

Our devotional Scripture for today is Matthew 20:26. But in order for us to fully understand it, we need to know what precedes it. In the previous verses Jesus told the twelve disciples that He would soon be betrayed, and the chief priests and scribes would condemn Him to death, turn Him over to the Romans, and He would be mocked and crucified, but afterward He will rise on the third day. Then the next verse tells us that the mother of James and John approached Jesus and requested that He promote her two sons so that one would sit on his right hand and the other on His left in his kingdom. Both were considered the highest positions of power next to a ruling king. The right hand is seen as the second in command and the left as the third.

Jesus had to remind the disciples, that even though the rulers of the world love to flaunt their authority over those they rule (20:25), He said His disciples would be different. Instead, any disciple of Christ who desired to be a leader must be a servant. Now, that is what being great is to Christ!

Food for Thought

Do you lord your leadership over those under your authority? _____
If so, what changes do you need to make? _____
_____
_____

➢ What ways can you be more servant-like?_____

_____

_____

➢ How do those you lead view you? Be honest with yourself. _____

_____

_____

_____

_____

Prayer

Father, thank you for the honor of serving You. Teach me how to be more like you so that humility shines through me and in my actions. Please lead me into how to effectively serve those you have entrusted me to lead. In Jesus' name, I pray. Amen.

Day Two

Handling Stress

> *Do not be anxious about anything, but in everything by prayer and supplication with thanksgiving let your requests be made known to God. And the peace of God, which surpasses all understanding, will guard your hearts and your minds in Christ Jesus.*
> ~Philippians 4:6–7 (ESV)

Stress is inward strain, pressure, tension, or anxiety, and it is a common occurrence for those in leadership. Besides all your other leadership responsibilities, more often than not, whenever you have to deal with people, there is a chance that your stress level will go up.

Our devotional Scripture for today encourages us to not worry about *anything.* That can be difficult, especially since most leaders tend to feel the need to shoulder everything. But Philippians 4:6–7 remind us that we have help and all we have to do is make our requests known to God. No matter how small or large, He can handle them. Of course, that does not mean that we relinquish our responsibilities, but we do our part and rely on God to do His. Trust that He will lead and guide us (Proverbs 3:5–6).

Effective leadership requires making hard choices and entails many obstacles. But perhaps one of the most difficult challenges you as a leader may face is waiting on God and trusting Him. Oh, I know we sing all the songs and say all the right things, but when it comes to actually doing it, do we trust God? Do we wait on Him? Or do we allow negative thoughts and doubts to flood our minds? Psalm 94:19 reminds us that when we are overwhelmed with thoughts and anxiety, we must learn to find comfort in God.

Stress can only consume us when we fully yield to it. But John 14:1 encourages us to not allow our hearts to be troubled; instead we are to trust in God. I know you may be thinking this is easier said than done, but the more time you spend with God, you will find yourself letting go of control, and listening carefully to His directions and responding accordingly.

Trusting God takes humility. We have to acknowledge that He is in control. Let's read 1 Peter 5:6–7 from the Amplified Bible:

> *Therefore humble yourselves <demote, lower yourselves in your own estimation> under the mighty hand of God, that in due time He may exalt you, Casting the whole of your care <all your anxieties, all your worries, all your concerns, once and for all> on Him, for He cares for you affectionately and cares about you watchfully.*

Food for Thought

So how do you as a leader handle stress?

➢ Always pray BEFORE moving forward with plans or ideas *(Is this what God wants you to do? Is this the season to do it? Have you counted the cost?)*

➢ Identify and know your stress triggers and learn what works best for you

➢ Delegate

➢ Know when to say no and do so without feeling guilty

➢ Seize opportunities to rest

➢ Learn to let go and trust God

Prayer

Father, thank you for entrusting so much into my care. I ask that you teach me how to be still and to know your voice. Let me hear you clearly so that the plans that I have are in alignment with your will for my life. Help me to let go of anything that is not in your plans for me so that I am a blessing to all those that I meet. Thank you for helping me to roll all of my cares into your hands. I choose to let go of anxiety over _____ because I trust you and know you are handling it and you know what is best. In Jesus' name, I pray. Amen.

Day Three

A Change Has To Come

To every thing there is a season, and a time to every purpose under the heaven. ~Ecclesiastes 3:1

C hange is inevitable and leaders' ability to initiate or adapt to change, as well as to lead others through change are paramount. If you have taken any college business classes, often Kodak is held up as the poster of a business whose leaders failed to adapt to change. What is strange is Kodak is credited with inventing the digital camera in 1975, years before others even imagined the capabilities. But the writing was on the wall. However, Kodak clung to what gave them their name—the old, which was film, while other companies slowly moved forward and then leaped into the digital age. Although Kodak did eventually move into the digital age, they lost the battle to smaller companies who responded to the demand for digital.

Effective leaders respond to the necessity of change, even if it requires letting go of what was always done. Efficient leaders never stop listening to others and refuse to become complacent. They do not ignore warning signs. Great leaders guide their people into necessary change, even if some rebel.

Our devotional Scripture today is a reminder that there is a season for every purpose that God has called us to do. We just need to know what season we are in and adapt accordingly. Knowing when to let go and when to hold on are two seasons that leaders must learn to discern.

Food for Thought

➤ What are you holding onto that God has asked you to let go? _____
_____
_____
_____
_____

➤ Why are you finding it difficult to move forward? _____

_____

_____

_____

➤ Have you let go of what God told you hold onto? _____ *(Sometimes out of fear, lack of support, discouragement, laziness, or insecurity, etcetera, we make a change before it is the season to do so)*

Basic Tips on Handling Change

➤ Observations should be made before you attempt to change things

➤ Take the people with you when making changes *(leaders have a responsibility to prepare those under their leadership regarding pending changes)*

➤ Do not think that just because the first attempt to bring about a necessary change did not work, that you should not revisit it after determining what hindered the initial attempt

➤ Recognize that the more you involve the people in each stage of the change, the greater the possibility of a smooth transition

➤ Change can sometimes be difficult, while at other times it can be comforting

Prayer

Father, I thank you for the strength and courage to lead your people. Help me to be sensitive to your voice so that I hear you clearly and do not miss your guidance. I ask for wisdom and understanding and that you help me to make the necessary changes to:

_____.

(list the changes)

Father, your Word declares that you know the thoughts and plans that you have for us, plans that are meant to prosper us and to give us a future and hope (Jeremiah 29:11). Lord, help us to embrace every season change you usher us into and to be content where you plant us. In Jesus' name. Amen.

Day Four

When Quitting is Not an Option

And let us not be weary in well doing: for in due season we shall reap, if we faint not. ~Galatians 6:9

Sometimes being a leader can be discouraging. But there are ample resources and insights available to help us to not get stuck in a rut of discouragement. For example, David's life provides us with a wealth of examples on an array of topics on leadership. This is why when I look at the subject of today's devotion, I immediately think of David at Ziglag when his men wanted to stone him.

And David was greatly distressed, for the people spoke of stoning him because the soul of all the people was grieved, every man for his sons and for his daughters; but David encouraged himself in the LORD his God. ~1 Samuel 30:6

This scene occurred before David was king. He was on the run from King Saul, who had become jealous of David because he knew that God had anointed David to be the next king. David had fled to Ziglag and many men with their families had also followed him.

One day David and his army were out on a mission and the Amalekites invaded the area where the women and children were and took them captive. When David and the men returned and saw that they had been raided and their families taken hostage, the men immediately turned on David and wanted to stone him.

Abandonment, betrayal, blame, being misunderstood, and so much more can be a day in a leader's life. David never asked them to follow him. He was originally hiding in a cave from Saul and the people sought out David and began to follow him. Being the leader that he is, he rose to the occasion. He did everything he could to protect them, ensure they had food and shelter, but the moment a crisis arose, they blamed David.

Leaders can have discouraging days and times when quitting seems to be the best option. However, when God has called you to a specific purpose, quitting is not an option, because your quitting will only means you will more than likely have to go through the same lesson somewhere else down the road.

David could have quit. He was abandoned by all those he had been leading. Can you imagine the scene? David's family had been taken captive just like the others' but his people could only feel their grief. So the leader in David rose up and he turned not to the men for support, but to God for encouragement.

As a leader, you will have days and even weeks when you feel like quitting. But you must step back from the situation and turn to God. Every leader should have contingency plans in place. This includes factoring in which Scriptures to flood your atmosphere for days when your most trusted church member or colleague betrays you, or a lie is seemingly prevailing, or whatever the trial is, and only a Word from God can shift you out of that dry place. You need to have Scriptures and songs set aside, be it in a folder on your electronic device or the old fashion writing pad. You need to have those songs already programmed so with a touch of a button or playing them on a disc, you can encourage yourself in the Lord.

One of my favorite Scriptures is Numbers 23:19:

> *God is not man, that he should lie, or a son of man, that he should change his mind. Has he said, and will he not do it? Or has he spoken, and will he not fulfill it?* (ESV)

Food for Thought

➢ List at least four Scripture references that you as leader find encouraging

_____

_____

_____

_____

➢ What are three songs that no matter how much you feel like quitting can encourage you to go another round?

_____

_____

_____

_____

➤ God has a purpose for you. Do you know what He has called you to do?

_____

_____

_____

_____

_____

_____

_____

_____

➤ Sometimes we feel like quitting because we are not in the place God has called us. Are you in the place that God has called to be and if not, what do you need to do get there? _____

_____

_____

_____

_____

_____

_____

_____

_____

_____

_____

When you come to the end of your
rope, tie a knot and hang on.
~Franklin D. Roosevelt

Prayer

Father, your Word tells me in Isaiah 40:31 that they who wait for the Lord shall renew their strength; they shall mount up with wings like eagles; they shall run and not be weary; they shall walk and not faint. I thank you for the strength to stay the course and for the courage to stand still.

I pray that you will bless all those under my leadership and strengthened them to not be moved by fear, anxiety, frustration, or whatever the enemy my devise to discourage them. Let us be united in purpose and fulfill our God-given mission. In Jesus' name I pray. Amen.

Making Tough Decisions

If any of you lacks wisdom, let him ask God, who gives generously to all without reproach, and it will be given him. But let him ask in faith, with no doubting, for the one who doubts is like a wave of the sea that is driven and tossed by the wind. For that person must not suppose that he will receive anything from the Lord; he is a double-minded man, unstable in all his ways.
~James 1:5–8 (ESV)

Leaders frequently have to make tough decisions, some of which may not be well received by others. This is why we as leaders must remember to always seek God for the what, how, when, and who.

Today's devotional passages tell us that when we use our faith and ask God for wisdom, He will give it to us so we are able to make decisions with confidence that all will be well, even as we maneuver through the challenges.

Leaders must begin each day with a consultation with God. This is the most important meeting of your day. There may also be a need for another such meeting as your day progresses. No matter how hectic your schedule is, you do not want to miss the opportunity to meet with the greatest counsel there is.

Frequently leaders may skip the daily consultation with the Father because getting leaders to sit still is often difficult, and to ask them to patiently wait on an answer is more than challenging. But Psalm 37:7 encourages us to be still before the Lord and to wait patiently on Him.

Why should we take the time to wait on the Lord—the great counselor? Because Proverbs 11:14 tells us:

> *Where no counsel is, the people fall;*
> *but in the multitude of counselors there*
> *is safety* (ESV).

If you have a tough decision, go to the Counselor. Proverbs 15:22 tells us that

"Without counsel purposes are disappointed, but in the multitude of counselors they are established." It is good to get sound input from your surrounding team members, but always make sure you have sought God so you will know how to discern the correct path to take.

> *Many are the plans in the mind of a man, but it is the purpose of the LORD that will stand.* ~Proverbs 19:21 (ESV)

Food for Thought

Scriptures and Quotes

➤ Psalm 16:7: I will bless the LORD, who has given me counsel: my reins also instruct me in the night seasons.

➤ Proverbs 12:15: The way of a fool is right in his own eyes: but he that listens to counsel is wise.

➤ Proverbs 19:2: Desire without knowledge is not good, and whoever makes haste with his feet misses his way (ESV).

➤ Proverbs 19:20: Hear counsel, and receive instruction, that you may be wise in your latter end.

➤ Proverbs 20:18: Every purpose is established by counsel: and with good advice make war.

➤ The hardest thing to learn in life is which bridge to cross and which to burn. ~David Russell

➤ Whatever course you decide upon, there is always someone to tell you that you are wrong. There are always difficulties arising which tempt you to believe that your critics are right. To map out a course of action and follow it to an end requires courage. ~Ralph Waldo Emerson

Prayer

Lord, give me the wisdom to know which path to take, which answer to give, who to appoint to what position, and when to move forward. Help those I lead to know and hear your voice. In Jesus' name I pray, Amen.

Day Six

Leading and Loving It

David retorted to Michal, "I was dancing before the LORD, who chose me above your father and all his family! He appointed me as the leader of Israel, the people of the LORD, so I celebrate before the LORD. ~2 Samuel 6:21 (NLT)

B eing a leader comes with a lot of responsibility. But the road to becoming a leader chosen by God usually entails many trials, and David's route was no different. When you have an opportunity, spend some time reading 2 Samuel and see how David became king.

At times, being *the* leader can be lonely, challenging, and even disheartening. However, we as leaders must remember that in the presence of the Lord is the fullness of joy (Psalm 16:11). I do not know where you are in your leadership journey, but I pray that you reach the stage where you love leading. Psalm 16:11 is one of the keys to getting to a place where leading is no longer a burden. The more time you spend in God's presence, the less impact the trials that often accompany leadership will have on you.

When we read our devotional Scripture, 2 Samuel 6:21, we can visualize the image of King David dancing in the streets, worshipping God, and celebrating the victory of having the ark of the Lord returned to them. We see a man leading and loving it. Although, his wife was offended by David's public worship display, David had reached a place in his leadership role where his joy was abundant and he did not care who saw it.

Being a leader is not easy. But I cannot stress enough the importance of spending time with the Father. Allow Him to chip away those things that hinder your leadership. Be quick to forgive. Do not hold grudges. Do not backbite. Refuse to tear down others, even when they have wronged you. Stay focused on your God-given mission and trust God.

It is an honor to be chosen and it can be a great joy. When God places you somewhere and you feel overwhelmed, get in His presence, speak His Word, follow His guidance, and watch Him work it out.

Food for Thought

> Take a moment and examine how you feel about your current leadership role. Are you loving it or looking for a way out? _____

_____

> Are you spending daily time in God's presence (prayer)? If not, what adjustments do you need to make to your schedule to ensure you do? ____

_____

_____

_____

Scriptures and Quotes

> Deuteronomy 31:8: And the LORD, he it is that does go before you; he will be with you, he will not fail you, neither forsake you: fear not, neither be dismayed.

➤ Joshua 4:14: That day the LORD made Joshua a great leader in the eyes of all the Israelites, and for the rest of his life they revered him as much as they had revered Moses.

➤ Psalm 145:14: The LORD upholds all that fall, and raises up all those that be bowed down.

➤ Psalm 51:12: Restore to me the joy of your salvation; and uphold me with your free spirit.

Prayer

Father, thank you for trusting me with the responsibility of being a leader. Teach me how to be a leader that pleases you. Help me to always walk in love and to hold no grudges. Lord, I choose to forgive and to not harbor ill feelings.

Lord, I worship you, and know that the more I am in your presence, my joy will be full and I will be strengthened. Let all those I lead be blessed and I ask that you empower them to be all that you have called them to be.

Loving People

And the Lord make you to increase and abound in love one toward another, and toward all men, even as we do toward you: To the end he may establish your hearts blameless in holiness before God, even our Father, at the coming of our Lord Jesus Christ with all his saints. ~I Thessalonians 3:12–13

The adage to do what I say and not what I do definitely does not apply when it comes to you as a leader loving those God has called you to lead. Being a leader requires a love for people. If we are honest with ourselves, love is the key to all relationships and leading people is much too demanding to accomplish without it.

In our devotional Scriptures Apostle Paul is asking that the Lord cause those in the church at Thessalonica to increase and abound in love toward all men. But he also puts himself and the other elders at Thessalonica before them as the example of showing love.

Food for Thought

Scriptures

➢ Psalm 109:4: In return for my love they accuse me, but I give myself to prayer (ESV).

➢ Matthew 5:44: But I say to you, Love your enemies, bless them that curse you, do good to them that hate you, and pray for them which spitefully use you, and persecute you.

➢ John 13:34–35: A new commandment I give to you, That you love one another; as I have loved you, that you also love one another. By this shall all men know that you are my disciples, if you have love one to another.

➢ 1 Peter 5:1–4: So I exhort the elders among you, as a fellow elder and a witness of the sufferings of Christ, as well as a partaker in the glory that is going to be revealed: shepherd the flock of God that is among you, exercising oversight, not under compulsion, but willingly, as God would have you; not for shameful gain, but eagerly; not domineering over those in your charge, but being examples to the flock. And when the chief Shepherd appears, you will receive the unfading crown of glory (ESV).

➢ Hebrews 6:10: For God is not unrighteous to forget your work and labor of love, which you have showed toward his name, in that you have ministered to the saints, and do minister.

➢ 1 John 3:16–18: By this we know love, that he laid down his life for us, and we ought to lay down our lives for the brothers. But if anyone has the world's goods and sees his brother in need, yet closes his heart against him, how does God's love abide in him? Little children, let us not love in word or talk but in deed and in truth (ESV).

[31]

> ➤ 1 John 4:7–8: Beloved, let us love one another, for love is from God, and whoever loves has been born of God and knows God. Anyone who does not love does not know God, because God is love (ESV).

Prayer

Lord, your Word says that your love has been poured out in our hearts through the Holy Spirit, so help me to allow this love to manifest in and through me so that I continuously walk in love. Help me to not be easily offended and to not keep count of the wrongs done to me. Lord, help me to be sensitive to the needs of others and to be aware when I have offended others.

Father, I pray that those I lead come to know the depth of your love for them and allow that love to saturate them and overflow into every area of their lives, so much so that they too will walk in love.

A Fresh Start

So when they had dined, Jesus said to Simon Peter, Simon, son of Jonas, love you me more than these? He said to him, Yes, Lord; you know that I love you. He said to him, Feed my lambs. He said to him the third time, Simon, son of Jonas, love you me? Peter was grieved because he said to him the third time, Love you me? And he said to him, Lord, you know all things; you know that I love you. Jesus said to him, Feed my sheep. ~John 21:15,17

Starting over can be scary, but there are times when it is absolutely necessary. As a leader you may find yourself in need of a fresh start. Perhaps you have had a failed business, or a ministry project that did not go well. You possibly may be emerging from the effects of a bad decision. If you are a pastor, maybe you are recovering from a church split. Or perchance you are still reeling from a failed marriage, as well as its impact on how others view you because of that.

Whatever the reason, you have nothing to fear from the need to have a fresh start. Our devotional Scriptures give us a glimpse of an interaction between Christ and Peter. It was after Peter had denied Christ three times and after the resurrection.

Can you imagine how Peter felt? He had walked with Jesus for the length of Jesus' public earthly ministry. When time grew near for the Crucifixion, Jesus pulled the disciples aside and told them that because of what was about to transpire that He knew they would all desert Him before the night was over (Matthew 26:31). However, Peter insisted that even though all the other disciples may leave Jesus, he would never turn his back on Him (Matthew 26:33). To which Jesus replied that Peter will deny him three times that very night before the rooster crows. The word "deny" in this context means to "affirm that one has no acquaintance or connection with someone."

Of course Peter did not believe he was capable of doing such a thing, so he rejected what Jesus said and told Jesus that he would never deny Him, in fact he said he would die with Jesus (Matthew 26:35). He was so adamant about this that when the soldiers came to take Jesus, Peter cut off the right ear of the high priest's servant (John 18:10). Peter also said he was ready to go with Jesus to prison and to death (Luke 22:33).

Yet, when the time came, Peter did not just deny Christ three times, he became angry at the mere question that he had any connection with Jesus. Mark 14:71 says "*But he began to curse and to swear, saying, I know not this man of whom you speak.*"

After the third denial and then hearing the rooster we are told that Peter wept bitterly (Luke 22:62). So now I want you to read again our devotional Scriptures for today. Do you see what Christ did after the resurrection? He went to the disciples and He ministered to Peter. He knew Peter was broken and felt horrible for what transpired. So Jesus gently restored Peter. He asked him three times if he loved Him—the same number of times that Peter had denied Christ. At first Peter may have thought it was a form of accusation, but it was restoration. Jesus told Peter to go and feed His lambs and His sheep.

Food for Thought

Maybe you feel that you have disappointed Christ in some way. But look at the love and patience Christ had with Peter as He restored him. Peter was given a fresh start. Jesus had promised Peter this even before Peter's denials:

> And the Lord said, Simon, Simon, behold, Satan has desired to have you, that he may sift you as wheat: But I have prayed for you, that your faith fail not: and when you are converted, strengthen your brothers (Luke 22:31–32).

God knows everything about us. And just like He prayed for Peter, He is making intercessions for you (Hebrews 7:25). You can start again. Let nothing deter you from starting fresh.

There are times when those who consider themselves too old to start again choose to not do so. But I encourage you to study the life of Moses and Joshua. At the age of 40 Moses believed it was his time to emerge from Pharaoh's house and go and see about his Hebrew brothers. But it did not go as he planned. The end result was Moses hiding on the backside of the desert for 40 years. Then at the age of 80 he had his burning bush experience (Acts 7:30) and emerged as the God-appointed deliverer for Israel, proving it is never too late to make a fresh start.

➤ Is there an area in your life where you need to make a fresh start? _____ If yes, what are some of the things you need to do to accomplish this? _____

_____

_____

_____

_____

What is your plan to do this? _____

_____

_____

_____

_____

_____

_____

_____

Scriptures

➤ Genesis 18:14: Is any thing too hard for the LORD? At the time appointed I will return to you, according to the time of life, and Sarah shall have a son.

➢ Isaiah 43:19: Behold, I will do a new thing; now it shall spring forth; shall you not know it? I will even make a way in the wilderness, and rivers in the desert.

➢ Lamentations 3:22–23: It is of the LORD's mercies that we are not consumed, because his compassions fail not. They are new every morning: great is your faithfulness.

➢ Jeremiah 32:27: Behold, I am the LORD, the God of all flesh: is there any thing too hard for me?

Prayer

Father, I thank you for being merciful and longsuffering. Thank you for setting before me an open door that no man can shut (Rev. 3:8). I ask that you order my steps (Ps. 37:23; 119:133), help me to not allow fear to prevent me from starting again. Bless all those I encounter and those under my leadership. Let us all seize every moment to please you and refuse to be bound by our past. In Jesus name I pray. Amen.

Leadership Growth

As long as a person doesn't know what he doesn't know, he doesn't grow.
~John Maxwell

There are times when people do not think of themselves as leaders and yet each of us possess one the most important keys to leadership—influence. According to John Maxwell, most people influence at least four people in the course of a day. Sometimes this is done purposefully or often without us even realizing it.

So even if you do not consider yourself a leader, you must be aware of your scope of influence because every leader has it in varying degrees. The more mindful you are of your impact on others, the more likely you are to increase your effectiveness as a leader as you mature in your leadership and become keenly aware of those who are following your guidance.

We are given a great opportunity to read of Joshua's growth as a leader under the guidance of Moses. We can trace his steps and see his maturation as a God-fearing leader.

Food for Thought

Scriptures

➢ Numbers 11:28: And Joshua the son of Nun, the servant of Moses, one of his young men, answered and said, My lord Moses, forbid them.

➢ Exodus 17:14: And the LORD said unto Moses, Write this for a memorial in a book, and rehearse it in the ears of Joshua: for I will utterly put out the remembrance of Amalek from under heaven.

➢ Exodus 24:13: And Moses rose up, and his minister Joshua: and Moses went up into the mount of God.

➢ Numbers 27:18: And the LORD said

unto Moses, Take thee Joshua the son of Nun, a man in whom is the spirit, and lay thine hand upon him;

➤ Numbers 27:22–23: And Moses did as the LORD commanded him: and he took Joshua, and set him before Eleazar the priest, and before all the congregation. And he laid his hands upon him and gave him a charge, as the LORD commanded by the hand of Moses.

➤ Deuteronomy 3:21: And I commanded Joshua at that time, saying, Thine eyes have seen all that the LORD your God hath done unto these two kings: so shall the LORD do unto all the kingdoms whither thou passest.

➤ Deuteronomy 3:28: But charge Joshua, and encourage him, and strengthen him: for he shall go over before this people, and he shall cause them to inherit the land which thou shalt see.

➤ Deuteronomy 34:9: And Joshua the son of Nun was full of the spirit of wisdom, for Moses had laid his hands upon him: and the children of Israel hearkened unto him, and did as the

LORD commanded Moses.

➢ Joshua 3:7–8: And the LORD said unto Joshua, "This day will I begin to magnify thee in the sight of all Israel, that they may know that, as I was with Moses, so I will be with thee. And thou shalt command the priests who bear the ark of the covenant, saying, 'When ye have come to the brink of the water of the Jordan, ye shall stand still in the Jordan.'"

Prayer

Lord, thank you for seeing me as you created me. Open my eyes so that I may see me as you see me, a leader, chosen by you. Please strengthen me and teach me how to mature in my role as a leader so that I may be a blessing to all those within my sphere of leadership. In Jesus' name I pray. Amen.

Leaders Inspire

The mediocre teacher tells. The good teacher explains. The superior teacher demonstrates. The great teacher inspires. ~William Arthur Ward

To inspire means: to influence by example; to encourage someone by making them feel confident and eager to do something: to impel; to stimulate to action; and to motivate. All of which great leaders do—inspire.

Look at Deborah, one of Israel's judges mentioned in the book of Judges. It was her who moved Barak to action when he was too afraid to obey God in His commissioning of him to pursue Sisera, the captain of King Jabin's army of Canaan.

And she sent and called Barak the son of Abinoam out of Kedeshnaphtali, and said unto him, Hath not the LORD God

of Israel commanded, saying, Go and draw toward mount Tabor, and take with thee ten thousand men of the children of Naphtali and of the children of Zebulun? And I will draw unto thee to the river Kishon Sisera, the captain of Jabin's army, with his chariots and his multitude; and I will deliver him into thine hand. And Barak said unto her, If thou wilt go with me, then I will go: but if thou wilt not go with me, then I will not go. And Deborah said unto Barak, Up; for this is the day in which the LORD hath delivered Sisera into thine hand: is not the LORD gone out before thee? So Barak went down from mount Tabor, and ten thousand men after him. ~Judges 4:6–8, 14

Although Barak still wanted Deborah to accompany him on the battlefield, he did go. Her inspiration was invaluable in moving him beyond his inaction. As a leader, you must know how, when, and what type of motivation is needed for your team to progress, because you never want those entrusted to your leadership to become stuck, stagnated, or to disengage from the mission.

To lead people, walk beside them. As for the best leaders, the people do not notice their existence.... When the best leader's work is done, the people say, 'We did it ourselves!' ~Lao Tzu

Food for Thought

As a leader, what are some things that you can do to inspire those you lead so they can mature in their gifts and purpose?

_____

_____

_____

_____

_____

_____

_____

_____

_____

Scriptures and Quotes

➢ The task of the leader is to get his people from where they are to where they have not been. ~Henry Kissinger

➢ Our chief want is someone who will inspire us to be what we know we could be. ~Ralph Waldo Emerson

➢ The final test of a leader is that he leaves behind him in other men, the conviction and the will to carry on. ~Walter Lippmann

➢ 1 Samuel 25:13: And David said unto his men, Gird ye on every man his sword. And they girded on every man his sword; and David also girded on his sword: and there went up after David about four hundred men; and two hundred abode by the stuff.

Prayer

Father, thank you for the Holy Spirit who leads, guides, and compels me to fulfill my God-given purpose. I pray that you equip me to know how to lead those you have assigned to my leadership so that I may inspire them to be the best they can be as they accomplish what you have called them to do. In Jesus' name I pray. Amen.

Day Eleven

Dealing with Rebellious People

When a country is rebellious, it has many rulers, but a ruler with discernment and knowledge maintains order. ~Proverbs 28:2 (NIV)

One aspect of leadership that every leader will encounter at least once is a rebellious person. But what is rebellion? It is important that leaders know how to identify rebellion so those who genuinely are seeking clarification are not labeled as rebellious.

Rebellion means: unwilling to obey rules or accept normal standards of behavior, dress, etcetera; deliberately not obeying people in authority; defying or resisting some established authority, government, or tradition. This is exactly what we read about

Korah's family in Numbers 16 when they led a rebellion against Moses' leadership.

> *Korah son of Izhar, the son of Kohath, the son of Levi, and certain Reubenites—Dathan and Abiram, sons of Eliab, and On son of Peleth—became insolenta and rose up against Moses. With them were 250 Israelite men, well-known community leaders who had been appointed members of the council. They came as a group to oppose Moses and Aaron and said to them, "You have gone too far! The whole community is holy, every one of them, and the Lord is with them. Why then do you set yourselves above the Lord's assembly?"*~Numbers 16:1–3 (NIV)

How you, the leader, respond to the rebellious is important, because you must choose to either trust God and follow His lead, or to take it personal and respond from a place of hurt and/or anger. Moses chose to trust God.

No doubt, each situation is different and requires prayer and guidance to know how to deal with the rebellious. Therefore, before you do anything you have to pray and listen for the Holy Spirit's leading. Then you must respond accordingly, because ignoring the issue is not an option. God is a God of order and clearly instructs us in Romans 12:18 "If it be possible, as much as lies in you, live peaceably with all men." Obviously there are some who may refuse to live peaceably with your leadership, just as Korah and his followers refused to peaceably submit to Moses' authority. Nonetheless, leaders are never to respond from a place of anger or with the agenda of getting even. Keep your motives pure and your heart open to reconciliation, but also take the necessary steps to protect others within your leadership from being wounded because of someone else's rebellion.

Often rebellion occurs when purpose is lost or forgotten. We must consistently remind the team of the vision and mission. Now, if you have just been doing for the sake of doing, then you may have a hard time restoring order. Go back to the basics. What is the purpose of your ministry or business? Foundation is important and if you need to start from scratch, then do so and build a solid foundation.

I encourage you to also study how David handled the rebellion of his men when they all wanted to stone him (1 Samuel 30). He acknowledged that he heard them and he did not respond in anger. But he immediately restored focus to the mission at hand and distracted them from their rebellion by pointing them to purpose. Another great example to examine is how Apostle Paul ministered to the church at Corinth who continuously challenged his authority as an apostle (2 Corinthians 10). One of the most important lessons is that Apostle Paul reminds us that the war is not against flesh and blood.

Food for Thought

Scriptures and Quotes

➢ Isaiah 63:10: But they rebelled against him and grieved his Holy Spirit. So he became their enemy and fought against them (NLT).

➢ You say, "Well, I am not going to be anyone's 'yes man.' If I see something wrong in a person, I'm going to warn others about it." Fine. But beware that what you are calling "courage to speak out" is not more truly a deception masking a rebellious, dishonoring attitude. ~Francis Frangipane

➤ Psalm 68:6: God places the lonely in families; he sets the prisoners free and gives them joy (NLT).

➤ Persistence in prayer for someone whom we don't like, however much it goes against the grain to begin with, brings about a remarkable change in attitude. ~F. F. Bruce

➤ An attitude can murder just as easily as an axe. ~Woodrow Knoll

➤ Ezra 4:19: And I commanded, and search hath been made, and it is found that this city of old time hath made insurrection against kings, and that rebellion and sedition have been made therein.

➤ 1 Samuel 15:23: For rebellion is as the sin of witchcraft, and stubbornness is as iniquity and idolatry. Because thou hast rejected the word of the LORD, he hath also rejected thee from being king.

➤ God uses broken things. It takes broken soil to produce a crop, broken clouds to give rain, broken grain to give bread, broken bread to give strength. It is the broken alabaster box that gives forth perfume. It is Peter, weeping bitterly, who returns to greater power than ever. ~Vance Havner

➢ Recommended reading:

  o "A Tale of Three Kings" by Gene Edwards (www.Amazon.com)

  o "Leading God's People Baggage Free" by Pamela Smith (www.TurningPointStore.org)

Prayer

Lord, teach me how to effectively minister to the rebellious and help me guide them into your light so that they may be restored and not miss the mark. Thank you for empowering me to not take it personally but to rise above the opposition and see your plan and purpose so I do not become sidetracked or bitter. In Jesus' name I pray. Amen.

Leaders Get Everyone Involved

The very essence of all power to influence lies in getting the other person to participate mediocre teacher tells. ~Harry A. Overstreet

When it comes to being a leader, your influence is mandatory if the team is to function as one. Therefore, you must know how to use your influence to get everyone involved in the vision. If you are unsure how to do this, spend some time studying the book of Nehemiah. It is a phenomenal study of leadership guiding team members in connecting to and fulfilling the vision, as well as overcoming oppositions.

The book of Nehemiah walks readers through how Nehemiah's influence inspired and awakened a nation to rise and build from the rubbles.

> *Then said I to them, You see the distress that we are in, how Jerusalem lies waste, and the gates thereof are burned with fire: come, and let us build up the wall of Jerusalem, that we be no more a reproach. Then I told them of the hand of my God which was good on me; as also the king's words that he had spoken to me. And they said, Let us rise up and build. So they strengthened their hands for this good work.* ~Nehemiah 2:17–18

Food for Thought

Scriptures and Quotes

➢ If your actions inspire others to dream more, learn more, do more and become more, you are a leader. ~John Adams

➢ People ask the difference between a leader and a boss. The leader leads, and the boss drives. ~Theodore Roosevelt

➤ No man will make a great leader who wants to do it all himself or get all the credit for doing it. ~Andrew Carnegie

➤ Nehemiah 4:14–18: And I looked, and rose up, and said to the nobles, and to the rulers, and to the rest of the people, Be not you afraid of them: remember the LORD, which is great and terrible, and fight for your brothers, your sons, and your daughters, your wives, and your houses. And it came to pass from that time forth, that the half of my servants worked in the work, and the other half of them held both the spears, the shields, and the bows, and the habergeons; and the rulers were behind all the house of Judah. They which built on the wall, and they that bore burdens, with those that laded, every one with one of his hands worked in the work, and with the other hand held a weapon. For the builders, every one had his sword girded by his side, and so built. And he that sounded the trumpet was by me.

> ➢ The leader can never close the gap between himself and the group. If he does, he is no longer what he must be. He must walk a tightrope between the consent he must win and the control he must exert. ~Vince Lombardi

Prayer

Lord, I pray for the wisdom to delegate, the patience to allow team members to learn, the understanding to make room for mistakes, and the humility to celebrate team members whose gifts and talents eventually surpass mine.

Thank you for allowing me the opportunity to lead such great people, and remove anything in me that hinders me from seeing them as you see them. Let me always bring out the best in them.

Day Thirteen

Working Through Mistakes

Though they stumble, they will never fall, for the LORD holds them by the hand. ~Psalm 37:24

D o you know that as long as you trust God there is no storm that you cannot endure or overcome? No matter how tumultuous it is, or even if it is a storm of your making, God is full of mercy and grace and Psalm 107:29 tells us "He makes the storm a calm, so that the waves thereof are still." You only need to have the courage to move through the storm and beyond your mistakes.

Sometimes leaders make mistakes that cause them to doubt themselves or feel unworthy of the position, but what does the Word say? Psalm 103:8 says that "The LORD is merciful and gracious, slow to anger, and plenteous in mercy." There is nothing too hard for God (Gen. 18:14; Jer. 32:17, 27). You must trust in His mercy and allow your heart to rejoice in His salvation (Ps. 13:5). Learn from your mistakes, forgive yourself, and raise your voice in song to Him, for He is the God of mercy and He is your defense (Ps. 59:16–17).

Food for Thought

Scriptures and Quotes

➢ As a leader, you must always have at least one person you can have honest dialogue with so you are not alone and overwhelmed by negative thoughts pertaining to mistakes you have made. Ecclesiastes 4:10: For if they fall, the one will lift up his fellow: but woe to him that is alone when he falls; for he has not another to help him up.

➢ You build on failure. You use it as a stepping stone. Close the door on the past. You don't try to forget the mistake, but you don't dwell on it. You don't let it have any of your energy, or any of your time, or any of your space. ~Johnny Cash

➢ A man must be big enough to admit his mistakes, smart enough to profit from them, and strong enough to correct them. ~John C. Maxwell

➢ There is a fine balance between honoring the past and losing yourself in it. For example, you can acknowledge and learn from mistakes you made, and then move on and refocus on the now. It is called forgiving yourself. ~Eckhart Tolle

➢ Proverbs 24:16: For a just man falls seven times, and rises up again: but the wicked shall fall into mischief.

➢ James 1:2–4: My brothers, count it all joy when you fall into divers temptations; Knowing this, that the trying of your faith works patience. But let patience have her perfect work, that you may be perfect and entire, wanting nothing.

➢ 2 Peter 1:10: Why the rather, brothers, give diligence to make your calling and election sure: for if you do these things, you shall never fall.

➤ All men make mistakes, but only wise men learn from their mistakes. ~ Winston Churchill

➤ Even a mistake may turn out to be the one thing necessary to a worthwhile achievement. ~Henry Ford

➤ Isaiah 41:10: Fear you not; for I am with you: be not dismayed; for I am your God: I will strengthen you; yes, I will help you; yes, I will uphold you with the right hand of my righteousness.

Prayer

Father, I praise your name and thank You for your mercy and grace. Thanks for restoring me and leading me in the path of righteousness. I choose to move beyond my mistakes and to trust you. I know that in and of myself I am not worthy, but the blood of Christ covers me and my life is hidden in Him (Col. 3:3). So I give you praise and honor and worship you. Please help me to live my life full of purpose and not regrets, and in a manner that constantly brings glory to your name. In Jesus' name I pray. Amen.

Making It On Your Own?

I am not able to bear all this people alone, because it is too heavy for me.
~Numbers 11:14

Thinking you can make it on your own is one of the biggest errors a leader can make. As great of a leader Moses was, in the beginning stages of his leadership of Israel he made a common leadership error—doing everything himself and not getting others involved. It was not until Jethro, his father-in-law, visited him and explained that Moses was on a path that would lead to burnout (Exodus 18). Effective leaders know they cannot do it all alone, so they surround themselves with others that are equipped to help fulfill the mission. Please study Exodus 18 as Jethro taught Moses the importance of delegating and sharing responsibilities as a leader.

Food for Thought

Scriptures

➢ Exodus 18:14, 17–18: And when Moses' father-in-law saw all that he did to the people, he said, "What is this thing that you do to the people? why sit you yourself alone, and all the people stand by you from morning to evening? And Moses' father-in-law said to him, The thing that you do is not good. You will surely wear away, both you, and this people that is with you: for this thing is too heavy for you; you are not able to perform it yourself alone."

➢ Seek advice, but make sure it's from someone who has successfully handled mistakes or adversities. ~John Maxwell

Prayer

Lord, help me to not only recognize the importance of not going at it alone, but show me how to engage others in fulfilling our God-given assignments. In Jesus' name I pray. Amen.

Real Leadership

Managers help people see themselves as they are; Leaders help people to see themselves better than they are. ~Jim Rohn

Leadership is so much more than having a position, and real leaders are easily identified by others, even when they do not have a title. David was a shepherd hiding in a cave, but others saw and identified him as a leader, so much so that many left a king in a palace (Saul) and joined themselves with a shepherd in a cave (1 Samuel 22, 24).

Spend some time this week studying David's leadership, as well as Christ's earthly leadership displayed to the twelve disciples. Through them, you should be able to see more clearly what real leadership is and is not.

Food for Thought

Scriptures and Quotes

➤ A leader is one who knows the way, goes the way, and shows the way. ~John C. Maxwell

➤ A leader is one who sees more than others see, who sees farther than others see, and who sees before others see. ~Leroy Elmes

➤ 1 Samuel 22:2: And every one who was in distress, and every one who was in debt, and every one who was discontented, gathered themselves unto him. And he became a captain over them, and there were with him about four hundred men.

Prayer

Lord, show me how to lead those entrusted into my leadership. Let me effectively guide them in a way that fulfills each of our purposes and matures us in our walk with you. In Jesus' name I pray. Amen.

Willing to Serve to the End

If you faint in the day of adversity, your strength is small. ~Proverbs 24:10

Being a leader requires stamina. There will undoubtedly be times when thoughts of quitting bombard your mind, but that is when great leaders tap into inner resources, and more importantly, they follow David's example in 1 Samuel 30:6—get strength from the Lord. As shared in our Day Four devotional, "David encouraged himself in the LORD his God."

As a leader, you have to be able to handle challenges, criticism, sabotage, and even out right rebellion, because quitting is not an option. Efficient leaders know how to lead in the calm and in a storm.

Food for Thought

Scriptures and Quotes

➤ Anyone can hold the helm with the sea is calm. ~Publilius Syrus

➤ Difficulties mastered are opportunities won. ~Winston Churchill

➤ Psalm 50:15: And call on me in the day of trouble: I will deliver you, and you shall glorify me.

➤ Nahum 1:7: The LORD is good, a strong hold in the day of trouble; and he knows them that trust in him.

Prayer

Father, I trust you and know that your plans for me are sure, for the Word says your plans stand firm forever and your intentions can never be shaken (Ps. 33:11). So I refuse to quit, because I know you are faithful and will work out the plans for my life (Ps. 138:8). Strengthen me as I press forward, knowing you have me and will not allow me to fail. In Jesus' name I pray. Amen.

Day Eighteen

Rest

And he said to them, Come you yourselves apart into a desert place, and rest a while: for there were many coming and going, and they had no leisure so much as to eat. ~Mark 6:31

One principle that every balanced leader needs to heed to is that of "rest." We have two outstanding examples of just how important rest is: one from God and one from Christ. On the seventh day, after God finished creation, He rested and that day is called blessed because He rested. That is how important rest is. No matter how busy you are, you have to take a real break from work. Even Leonardo da Vinci knew this:

Every now and then go away, have a little relaxation, for when you come back to your work your judgment will be surer. Go some distance away because then the work appears smaller and more of it can be taken in at a glance and a lack of harmony and proportion is more readily seen.

Food for Thought

Scriptures

- ➤ Genesis 2:2–3: On the seventh day God had finished his work of creation, so he rested from all his work. And God blessed the seventh day and declared it holy, because it was the day when he rested from all his work of creation.

- ➤ 2 Samuel 16:14: The king and all who were with him grew weary along the way, so they rested when they reached the Jordan River.

Prayer

Lord, thanks for your wonderful example on the importance of rest. Help me to not get so lost in working that I neglect to seize times to just sit still. In Jesus' name I pray. Amen.

Day Nineteen

Handling Rejection

And the LORD said to Samuel, Listen to the voice of the people in all that they say to you: for they have not rejected you, but they have rejected me, that I should not reign over them. ~1 Samuel 8:7

There are times when you as a leader may be rejected. This can be very difficult to understand or forgive. However, if you are to successfully lead others, you must know that it comes with the territory, and failing to move beyond it can hamper your ability to effectively lead.

Do not allow being rejected to cause you to harbor unforgiveness or to become stuck. Pick yourself up and keep moving forward. Allow God to show you the bigger picture, like he did Samuel, whose leadership was rejected by the Israelites. Or even examine

Moses, who thought that his people would understand that he was called to be a ruler and judge over them, but he was rejected by his fellow Hebrew brothers. They asked, "Who made you a ruler and a judge over us?" (Acts 7).

You can also look at David, who was called to be king, but initially his leadership was rejected and the nation was divided. So David ruled Judah and Saul's family ruled Israel until eventually Israel accepted David's leadership (2 Sam. 6:21; 1 Chr. 11:1–3).

Furthermore, take an opportunity to do some background reading on Abraham Lincoln. Yes, he was the president of the United States, but before that he had several failed businesses, was rejected when he applied for law school, lost the first time he ran for state legislature, went bankrupt, had a nervous breakdown, lost several political elections including as an elector, congressman, and senator. His life was paved with numerous rejections, but each time he eventually picked himself up and kept moving toward his destiny. He obviously knew that one of the keys to overcoming rejection is to not take it personal so that it can gain no power over your forward movement.

Finally, spend time studying Christ's ministry. Not only was He rejected but He was brutalized and crucified (Isa. 53:3; Mk. 8:31; 12:10; Lk. 7:30). Yet, He never lost focus of the mission (Heb. 12:1–3) and neither should you. Instead, prepare yourself to handle rejection and refuse to give it undeserved space in your thoughts or allow it to paralyze you.

> *It is not rejection itself that people fear; it is the possible consequences of rejection. Preparing to accept those consequences and viewing rejection as a learning experience that will bring you closer to success, will not only help you to conquer the fear of rejection, but help you to appreciate rejection itself.*
> ~Robert Foster Bennett

Food for Thought

Scriptures and Quotes

➤ Success is buried on the other side of rejection. ~Tony Robbins

➤ You must learn how to handle rejection. To succeed, you must learn how to cope with a little word 'no', learn how to strip that rejection of all its power. The best salesmen are those who are rejected most. They are the ones who can take any 'no' and use it as a prod to go onto the next 'yes'. ~Tony Robbins

➤ Too many Christians have a commitment of convenience. They'll stay faithful as long as it's safe and doesn't involve risk, rejection, or criticism. Instead of standing alone in the face of challenge or temptation, they check to see which way their friends are going. ~Charles Stanley

➤ Rejection is the sand in the oyster, the irritant that ultimately produces the pearl. ~Bruce Wilkinson

Prayer

Father, I submit myself to your plan for my life and I refuse to allow rejection to consume me or hinder me from moving on the path you have set for me. I ask that you give me favor with others and continue to open a door that no man can close so I can be a blessing to those I encounter (Ps. 5:12; Prv. 3:4; Rev. 3:8). In Jesus' name I pray. Amen.

Day Twenty

God's Power in Your Weakness

And he said to me, My grace is sufficient for you: for my strength is made perfect in weakness. Most gladly therefore will I rather glory in my infirmities, that the power of Christ may rest on me. ~2 Corinthians 12:9

Just think, you have access to the greatest power in the world and all you have to do is call His name. No matter what time of day or night or what the circumstance, He is just a prayer away. Mention His name, and the heavens open up to you.

So how great it is to be a leader with a phenomenal connection that can transform a situation in a blink of an eye! This means that when you feel overwhelmed or even when you fall short, you have a resource that can step in and provide immediate assistance or deliverance, whatever is needed. All you have to do is trust God, admit you need Him, invite Him into your situation, and allow Him to intervene.

Food for Thought

Scriptures

➢ Psalms 18:2, 32: The LORD is my rock, and my fortress, and my deliverer; my God, my strength, in whom I will trust; my buckler, and the horn of my salvation, and my high tower. It is God that girds me with strength, and makes my way perfect.

➢ Psalm 73:26: My flesh and my heart fails: but God is the strength of my heart, and my portion for ever.

Prayer

Lord, you are my strength. It is you who empowers me to overcome and standfast and rise to be the leader you are calling me to be. I put my trust fully in you and I yield to your guidance. In Jesus' name I pray. Amen.

Leading Change

There is nothing more difficult to take in hand, more perilous to conduct, or more uncertain in its success, than to take the lead in the introduction of a new order of things. ~N. Machiavelli

Nothing tests a leader more than his or her ability to successfully guide the organization through change, and leaders who have accomplished this know that the foundation for moving any organization through change is trust. If the people do not trust you or your leadership you will encounter massive resistance.

Any leader who insists on making changes without first establishing a relationship built on trust will fail to navigate the people through the changes. Take David's leadership as king of Judah and then king of all Israel as a great example of a leader guiding his people through change. Initially there was great resistance from Israel, but in 2 Samuel 5 we read where all Israel eventually accepted the change because they had gotten to know and trust King David and his leadership.

Food for Thought

Scriptures and Quotes

➢ Leadership is the engine that drives change. ~John Kotter

➢ 2 Samuel 5:1–2: Then all the tribes of Israel went to David at Hebron and told him, "We are your own flesh and blood. In the past, when Saul was our king, you were the one who really led the forces of Israel. And the LORD told you, 'You will be the shepherd of my people Israel. You will be Israel's leader.'"

Prayer

Father, show me how to lead the people through the changes so that we stay united and focused, and bring glory to your name. In Jesus' name I pray. Amen.

Balancing Your Life

Beloved, I wish above all things that you may prosper and be in health, even as your soul prospers.
~3 John 1:2

Balance is a necessity for longevity and effectiveness in leadership. But what do we mean when we say we need to have a balanced life? Well, balance means: the ability to remain steady when you are standing up; stable position; steady; a state in which all your weight is evenly spread so that you do not fall; equal amounts; mental or emotional steadiness. So having a balanced life means you have purposefully and properly divided your time and energy in a manner in which you can efficiently and consistently withstand whatever you may encounter daily without losing focus or becoming emotionally unstable.

You do this by following Christ's advice given to Martha, who was so busy with her day-to-day responsibilities that even when face-to-face with Jesus she did not take the time to sit at His feet, and was frustrated that her sister Mary did:

> *But Martha was encumbered about much serving, and came to him, and said, Lord, do you not care that my sister has left me to serve alone? bid her therefore that she help me. And Jesus answered and said to her, Martha, Martha, you are careful and troubled about many things: But one thing is needful: and Mary has chosen that good part, which shall not be taken away from her.* ~Luke 10:40–42

Are you so busy that you have neglected your prayer life, family time, your health, personal Bible study time, worship time, your home, or even failing to take breaks or vacations? If so, you are not living a balanced life and need to start today to take the necessary steps to bring balance in your life or it may lead to exhaustion, burnout, family issues, or poor health, among some other issues.

So I encourage you to do a study of Colossians 3 and allow it to help you to pause and establish a realistic plan that will enable you to bring balance into your life.

Food for Thought

Make a list of what takes the most of your time daily, then the second most, and so forth. What can you adjust that will allow you to stop neglecting areas that need your attention in order to live a balanced life? _____

_____

_____

_____

_____

_____

Scriptures and Quotes

➤ Problems arise in that one has to find a balance between what people need from you and what you need for yourself. ~Jessye Norman

- ➢ To go beyond is as wrong as to fall short. ~Confucius

- ➢ The key to keeping your balance is knowing when you've lost it.

- ➢ I believe that being successful means having a balance of success stories across the many areas of your life. You can't truly be considered successful in your business life if your home life is in shambles.~Zig Ziglar

  - ➢ Life is a balance of holding on and letting go. ~Rumi

- ➢ Ecclesiastes 3:1: To every thing there is a season, and a time to every purpose under the heaven.

Prayer

Father, I worship you and give you praise. You alone are God and know the plans for my life. I pray that you reveal to me how to bring balance into my life so that I may fulfill my purpose and not neglect that which is needful for having a balanced life. Thanks for showing me the way. In Jesus' name I pray. Amen.

Day Twenty-Three

Moving Past Betrayal

A brother offended is harder to be won than a strong city: and their contentions are like the bars of a castle. ~Proverbs 18:19

There are times when a leader is betrayed or backstabbed and the leader does not move beyond the pain or disappointment of the incident. Although it is easier said than done, as a leader you must forgive and harbor no ill-will toward the betrayers.

Moving past the pain of betrayal is a process, but can be done. Look at the example of Jesus, who was betrayed by Judas (Lk. 22) and then His trusted disciple, Peter, three times denied knowing Jesus (Mt. 22). Another great example for you to study is David, who was betrayed by his son Absalom and eventually many other of his trusted leaders who helped Absalom temporarily overthrow David's leadership (2 Sam. 13–14, 18–19).

One thing that you must do no matter how deep the disappointment, is do not feed the pain you have by constantly thinking of the betrayal.

Food for Thought

Scriptures and Quotes

➢ Betrayal is advancing myself at the expense of the one who I committed myself to advance. ~Craig D. Lounsbrough

➢ Shattered legs may heal in time, but some betrayals fester and poison the soul. ~George Martin

➢ If you're betrayed, release disappointment at once. By that way, the bitterness has no time to take root. ~Toba Beta

➢ Matthew 5:44–47: But I say to you, Love your enemies, bless them that curse you, do good to them that hate you, and pray for them which spitefully use you, and persecute you; That you may be the children of your Father which is in heaven: for he makes his sun to rise on the evil and on the good, and sends rain on the just and on the unjust. For if you love them which love you, what reward have you? do not even the publicans the same? And if you salute your brothers only, what do you more than others? do not even the publicans so?

➤ Mark 11:25: And whenever you stand praying, if you have anything against anyone, forgive him and let it drop (leave it, let it go), in order that your Father Who is in heaven may also forgive you your <own> failings and shortcomings and let them drop (AMPC).

➤ Luke 6:28: Bless them that curse you, and pray for them which spitefully use you.

➤ Luke 22:48: But Jesus said to him, Judas, betray you the Son of man with a kiss?

➤ While stabbing someone's back, you recklessly expose your own. ~Matshona Dhilwayo

➤ Colossians 3:12–13: Put on therefore, as the elect of God, holy and beloved, bowels of mercies, kindness, humbleness of mind, meekness, long-suffering; Forbearing one another, and forgiving one another, if any man have a quarrel against any: even as Christ forgave you, so also do you.

➤ Psalm 34:18: The LORD is close to the brokenhearted; he rescues those whose spirits are crushed (NLT).

Prayer

Lord, release me from the pain of betrayal and heal my wound and do not allow it to take root in my heart. Heal my wounded spirit and cause me to soar far above the pain and disappointment as I release those who have wronged me and submit myself to your guidance. Let me not dwell on the incident, but instead saturate myself in your Word as I emerge victoriously. Bless others who may have been impacted by what happened and heal them. I forgive those who have wronged me and ask that you shine your light in their hearts. In Jesus' name I pray. Amen.

Day Twenty-Four

When It Seems God
Is Not Showing Up

God is our refuge and strength, a very present help in trouble. ~Psalm 46:1

G od is a present help in seasons of trouble. Although, I know at times even when we do cry out to God it may seem as if our cries are falling on deaf ears. I recall when I went through some tough storms and I wondered if God was watching or cared about my pain. But in the midst of it, I drew strength from what my parents taught me about God's unfailing love, and that tests and storms come our way but they do not mean God is not watching over us (Ps. 17:7; 31:7; 33:18; 105:16–22). Plus, Hebrews 13:5–6 say that God will never leave or forsake me, so I can boldly declare that "The Lord is my helper, and I will not fear what man shall do unto me." This is great news because at times even our friends or family may abandon us. But God is faithful and has never failed me. All we need to do is trust Him and wait on Him and we will reap and witness the benefits of His blessings. That is why one of my favorite Scriptures is Romans 8:28: "And we know that all things work together for good to them that love God, to them who are the called according to his purpose."

Food for Thought

Scripture

> James 1:3–4: Knowing this, that the trying of your faith works patience. But let patience have her perfect work, that you may be perfect and entire, wanting nothing.

Prayer

Father, I worship you and thank you for always being there. Great is your faithfulness to us. Let me be sensitive enough to hear your voice and help me to see your hand in my life and to not lose hope. In Jesus' name I pray. Amen.

Day Twenty-Five

Harmonizing the Team

The strength of the team is each individual member. The strength of each member is the team. ~Phil Jackson

Sometimes leading a team into harmony is a challenge. But as a leader, you are responsible for the unity of the team. So one of the first things you as leader need to do is ensure each member feels as if they belong. A sense of belonging will guide members into a feeling ownership, which is vital to maximum team production.

Psalm 133:1 declares "Behold, how good and how pleasant it is for brothers to dwell together in unity!" Then we are told that unity is like "the precious ointment on the head, that ran down on the beard, even Aaron's beard: that went down to the skirts of his garments." Finally, we read that unity is where the "Lord commanded the blessing..." (Ps. 133:3). So a unified team is a blessed team, this why you constantly want to lead your team into harmony and dissuade any division, no matter how small because if ignored it will only magnify.

Food for Thought

Scriptures

➢ 1 Corinthians 12:12: For as the body is one, and has many members, and all the members of that one body, being many, are one body: so also is Christ.

➢ Colossians 4:13: Above all, clothe yourselves with love, which binds us all together in perfect harmony.

Prayer

Father, thank you for the team you have entrusted me to lead. Show me how to develop and keep unity among them so that they may function as one harmonious unit. In Jesus' name I pray. Amen.

Day Twenty-Six

Edifying Your Team

*Therefore encourage (admonish, exhort)
one another and edify (strengthen and
build up) one another, just as you are
doing.* ~1 Thessalonians 5:11 (AMPC)

Do you want a strong team? Then
you need to contribute to building
the members up so they are fully
equipped to complete the vision
and mission. This is vital because the more
prepared the team is, the greater the
members' confidence, and this assurance
leads to members flowing as one.

As you take the time to pour into each
team member you not only build a stronger
relationship with them, you also help them
develop their skills, and every great leader
understands this necessity, even when it
seems that some are unappreciative. This is
why Apostle Paul said, "I will gladly spend

myself and all I have for you, even though it seems that the more I love you, the less you love me" (2 Cor. 12:15, NLT). He understood regardless of some of the members' responses, one of his responsibilities as a leader was to pour into them.

Food for Thought

Quotes

➢ The signs of outstanding leadership appear primarily among the followers. Are the followers reaching their potential? Are they learning? Serving? Do they achieve the required results? Do they change with grace? Manage conflict? ~Max de Pree

➢ Leadership is a serving relationship that has the effect of facilitating human development. ~Ted Ward

Prayer

Father, guide me in how to encourage and build up my team so they reach their fullest potential and bring glory to your name as they accomplish what You have called them to do. In Jesus' name I pray, Amen.

Leaders Raise Up Leaders

There is nothing worse for a young convert than to be thrust into leadership without mentoring and ongoing coaching because the devil relishes these vulnerable souls. ~Gary Rohrmayer

Y ou should not place a person in a leadership position just to fill a vacancy. You have to ensure the person has leadership abilities and that you the leader tap into those qualities, because as John Maxwell said, "Followers simply cannot develop leaders." Therefore, as the leader you must cultivate other leaders.

One of our greatest examples is Jesus and the twelve disciples. We read how He called each of the disciples, who all brought their individual strengths and Jesus molded them into apostles whose impact is still felt today. That is what leaders do—raise up other leaders. Study the ministry of Christ and notice how much time He spent pouring into the disciples, maturing their gifts. Read how He shaped fishermen, a doctor, a tax collector, and other tradesmen into ministry leaders that continued Christ's mission.

Food for Thought

Scriptures and Quotes

➢ Matthew 4:19: And he said to them, Follow me, and I will make you fishers of men.

➢ Leaders don't create followers, they create more leaders. ~Tom Peters

➢ Growing other leaders from the ranks isn't just the duty of the leader, it's an obligation. ~Warren Bennis

Prayer

Lord, let me be a leader that has vision and can easily identify the gifts of my team members and then show me the best way to nature and mature their leadership skills. In Jesus' name I pray. Amen.

Transformed by Truth

And be not conformed to this world: but be you transformed by the renewing of your mind, that you may prove what is that good, and acceptable, and perfect, will of God. ~Romans 12:2

God's Word is truth (Jhn. 1:14) and is powerful enough to transform the way we think and behave, as well as to guide us into His will. As such, it is a roadmap for success in leadership with its numerous examples of effectively leading people.

As you study this indispensable roadmap, you gain strength, clarity, and purpose as the light of the Word penetrates your heart. If you want to know what your next steps should be, turn to the Word. If you are feeling lost or want to give up, take a step back and study the Word. No matter what answers you seek, the Word can transform your confusion or lack of understanding into sound guidance.

Food for Thought

Scriptures and Quotes

➢ Acts 20:32: And now, brothers, I commend you to God, and to the word of his grace, which is able to build you up, and to give you an inheritance among all them which are sanctified.

➢ John 1:17: For the law was given by Moses, but grace and truth came by Jesus Christ.

➢ John 14:17: Even the Spirit of truth; whom the world cannot receive, because it sees him not, neither knows him: but you know him; for he dwells with you, and shall be in you.

Prayer

Lord, I yield to you and ask that your Word transform my thinking and guide me into leading your people in a manner that pleases you. In Jesus' name I pray, Amen.

[94]

Day Twenty-Nine

Transformed by Trouble

For our present troubles are small and won't last very long. Yet they produce for us a glory that vastly outweighs them and will last forever!
~2 Corinthians 4:17 (NLT)

It may not seem like trouble can bring about anything good, but God loves us enough to trust us with trouble. Just like He allowed Satan to test Job, we are no less important to Him (Job 1:8).

So often in church when someone goes through a trial, some automatically assumes the person has sinned or done something to deserve it. But just as Jesus explained to his disciples and the others who also thought this, it should not be an automatic notion (Jhn. 9: 1–3) since often the trial is an attack from Satan or a test to bring spiritual maturity or further growth.

[95]

Food for Thought

Scriptures and Quotes

➢ Genesis 50:20: But as for you, you thought evil against me; but God meant it to good, to bring to pass, as it is this day, to save much people alive.

➢ Our most significant opportunities will be found in times of greatest difficulty. ~Thomas S. Monson

➢ Joshua 2:21–22: I will no longer drive out the nations that Joshua left unconquered when he died. I did this to test Israel—to see whether or not they would follow the ways of the LORD as their ancestors did."

➢ We love being mentally strong, but we hate situations that allow us to put our mental strength to good use. ~Mokokoma Mokhonoana

➢ John 9:3: Jesus answered, Neither has this man sinned, nor his parents: but that the works of God should be made manifest in him.

> Deuteronomy 8:2: And you shall remember all the way which the LORD your God led you these forty years in the wilderness, to humble you, and to prove you, to know what was in your heart, whether you would keep his commandments, or no.

> Sometimes new opportunity means new opposition. Not everything God asks us to do will be comfortable. ~Joyce Meyer

> If you allow it, [suffering] can be the means by which God brings you His greatest blessings. ~Charles Swindoll

> 1 Corinthians 10:13: There has no temptation taken you but such as is common to man: but God is faithful, who will not suffer you to be tempted above that you are able; but will with the temptation also make a way to escape, that you may be able to bear it.

> 1 Peter 4:12-13: Beloved, think it not strange concerning the fiery trial which is to try you, as though some strange thing happened to you: But rejoice, inasmuch as you are partakers of Christ's sufferings; that, when his glory

shall be revealed, you may be glad also with exceeding joy.

➤ James 1:2–4: Dear brothers and sisters, when troubles come your way, consider it an opportunity for great joy. For you know that when your faith is tested, your endurance has a chance to grow. So let it grow, for when your endurance is fully developed, you will be perfect and complete, needing nothing (NLT).

Prayer

Lord, my life is in your hands and I trust you and know that you will cause all things to work for my good, because you will work out your plans for my life for your faithful love endures forever (Ps. 138:8). Thanks for giving me the strength to persevere and wait on you. Let me always see the big picture and not get lost in the pain of the trial because I am confident that no weapon formed against me shall prosper (Isa. 54:17). In Jesus' name I pray. Amen.

Necessity for Patience

Finishing is better than starting.
Patience is better than pride.
~Ecclesiastes 7:8

Patience is the capacity to tolerate delay, trouble, suffering, something disagreeable or inconvenient and to continue waiting for a long time without complaining, becoming angry, or losing focus. So, do you have patience?

Any leader can tell you there are no quick fixes; therefore, patience is a quality that every successful leader must have. Henri Nouwen, a Dutch priest, made a profound statement: "To learn patience is not to rebel against every hardship." This fits right into the definition of patience, because patience is not just about waiting, but how you wait.

Read 2 Corinthians 6:6 to see another important aspect about patience:

We prove ourselves by our purity, our understanding, our patience, our kindness, by the Holy Spirit within us, and by our sincere love (NLT).

We prove ourselves by our patience and it is a witness to our character. Just look at Apostle Paul whose patience was a testimony to his leadership and walk in Christ. When he wrote Timothy he said:

But you, Timothy, certainly know what I teach, and how I live, and what my purpose in life is. You know my faith, my patience, my love, and my endurance. ~2 Timothy 3:10 (NLT)

People know when you have patience and when you do not, and dependent upon where you stand on the patience thermometer, it will either positively or negatively impact your ability to lead.

Therefore, patience is vital to the health of your leadership so take some time to evaluate where you stand in this area. It is what helps keep you from making rash decisions, erratically reacting to crises, rushing into bad investments, using so-called quick fixes, and from bailing when you should stay.

Food for Thought

Scriptures and Quotes

➢ Teach us, O Lord, the disciplines of patience, for to wait is often harder than to work. ~Peter Marshall

➢ Patience is bitter, but its fruit is sweet. ~Jean-Jacques Rousseau

➢ Romans 15:5: May God, who gives this patience and encouragement, help you live in complete harmony with each other, as is fitting for followers of Christ Jesus.

➢ Galatians 5:22–23: But the Holy Spirit produces this kind of fruit in our lives: love, joy, peace, patience, kindness, goodness, faithfulness, meekness, temperance: against such there is no law.

➢ Colossians 1:11–12: We also pray that you will be strengthened with all his glorious power so you will have all the endurance and patience you need. May you be filled with joy, always thanking the Father. He has enabled you to share in the inheritance that belongs to his people, who live in the light (NLT).

➢ Titus 2:2: Teach the older men to exercise self-control, to be worthy of respect, and to live wisely. They must have sound faith and be filled with love and patience (NLT).

➢ James 5:10: For examples of patience in suffering, dear brothers and sisters, look at the prophets who spoke in the name of the Lord.

Prayer

Father, thank you for the Holy Spirit who leads, guides, and compels me to fulfill my God-given purpose. I pray that You equip me to know how to lead those You have assigned to my leadership so that I may inspire them to be the best they can be as they accomplish what You have called them to do. In Jesus' name I pray, Amen.

➢ I like a leader who can, while pointing out a mistake, bring up the good things the other person has done. If you do that, then the person sees that you have a complete picture of him. There is nobody more dangerous than one who has been humiliated, even when you humiliate him rightly. ~Nelson Mandela

➢ True leadership strengthens the followers. It is a process of teaching, setting an example, and empowering others. If you seek to lead, your ability will ultimately be measured in the successes of those around you. ~David Niven

➢ 1 Samuel 15:17: And Samuel told him, "Although you may think little of yourself, are you not the leader of the tribes of Israel? The LORD has anointed you king of Israel (NLT).

LaJoyce C. Harris

LaJoyce C. Harris is a minister of the Gospel and a gifted teacher of children, as well as creative in writing lesson plans for children. Since her youth she has used her gifts of reaching children, not just in her Sunday school classes but in her privately owned day care center.

She is the proud mother of two adult children, Yolanda (Patrick) and Justin and two wonderful grandsons.

Manufactured by Amazon.ca
Bolton, ON